This book belongs to:

Mrs. Sandfort

This one has become…

...a plum.

With love to Paul and Philip and Lisa

Special
thanks
to
Glenn Keator, Ph.D.
Director of Education
Strybing Arboretum Society
San Francisco, California

RUTH HELLER

WORLD OF NATURE

THE REASON
FOR A FLOWER

Written and illustrated by

RUTH HELLER

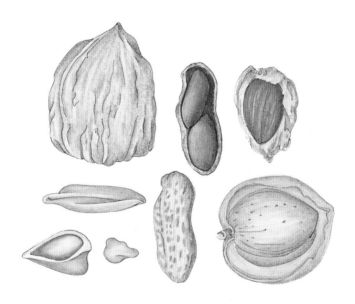

Penguin Putnam Books for Young Readers

Birds
and
bees,

and
these,

and
these
sip
NECTAR
from
the
FLOWERS.

And as they search
for more and more,
POLLEN
from the
flower before
goes…

to
the
next
one
they
explore.

Some POLLEN
travels
in
the
breeze,

without
the
help
of
birds
or
bees,
and
very
often
makes
you
sneeze.

From an ANTHER on a STAMEN

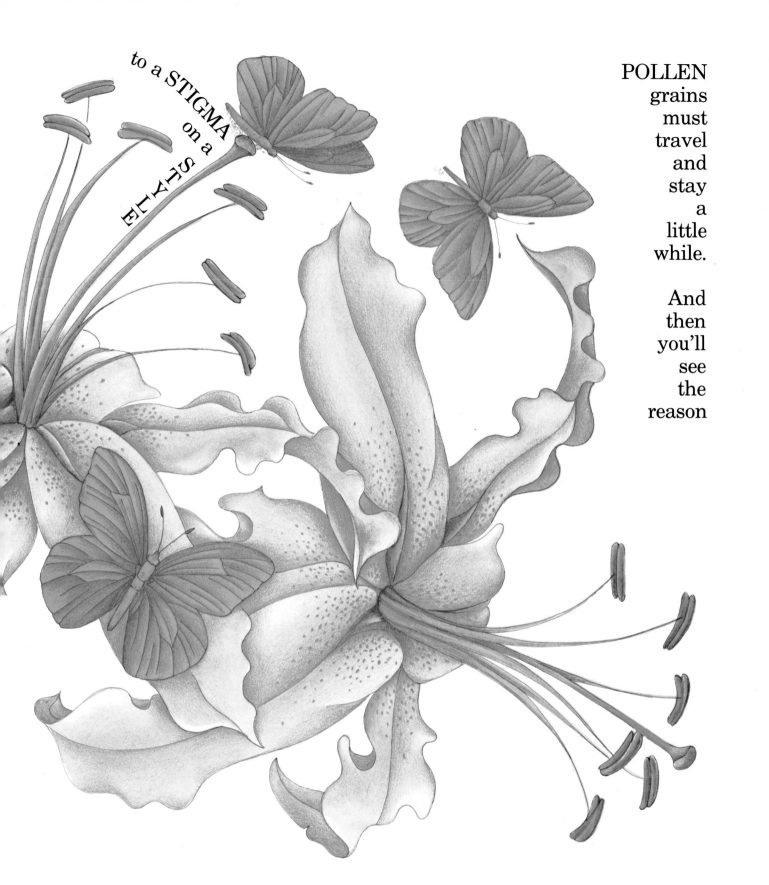

to a STIGMA on a STYLE

POLLEN grains must travel and stay a little while.

And then you'll see the reason

for each FLOWER—

even WEEDS.

The
reason
for
a
FLOWER
is
to
manufacture…

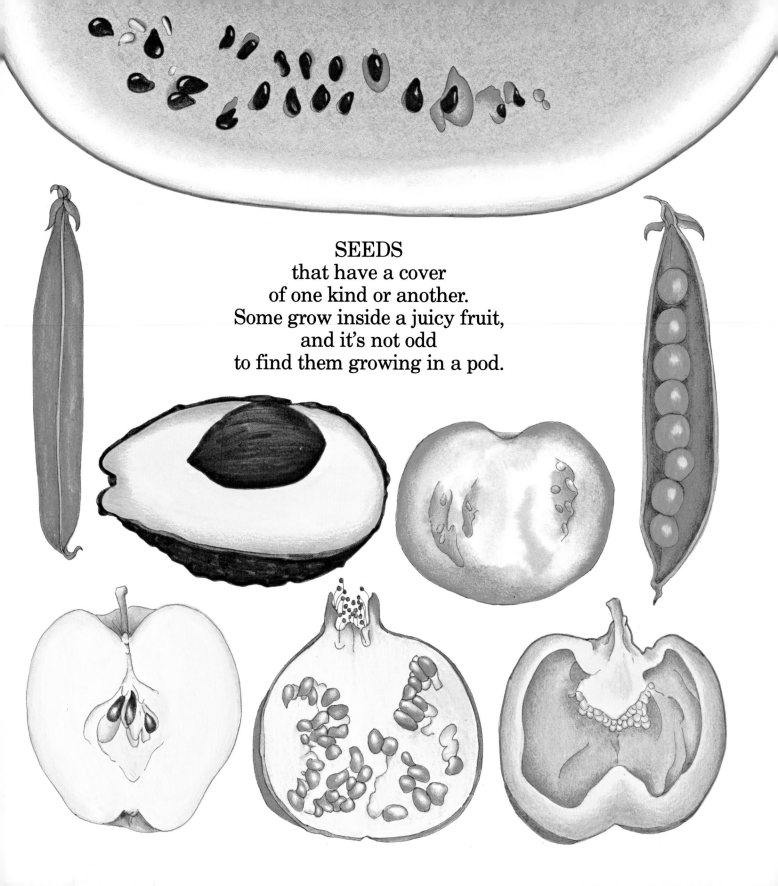

SEEDS
that have a cover
of one kind or another.
Some grow inside a juicy fruit,
and it's not odd
to find them growing in a pod.

The
largest
one's a COCONUT.

SEEDS travel far and wide. Some even like to hitch a ride upon a bike or on a shoe.

Squirrels hide them and forget they do.

Some have
burrs
that stick to furs
and
travel at a
gallop.

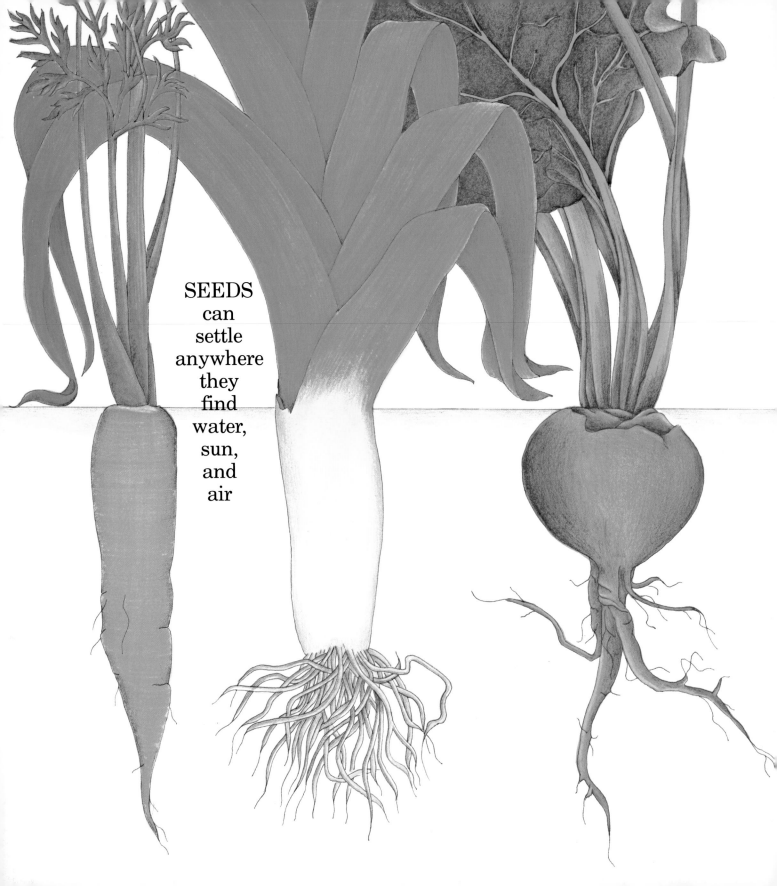

SEEDS
can
settle
anywhere
they
find
water,
sun,
and
air

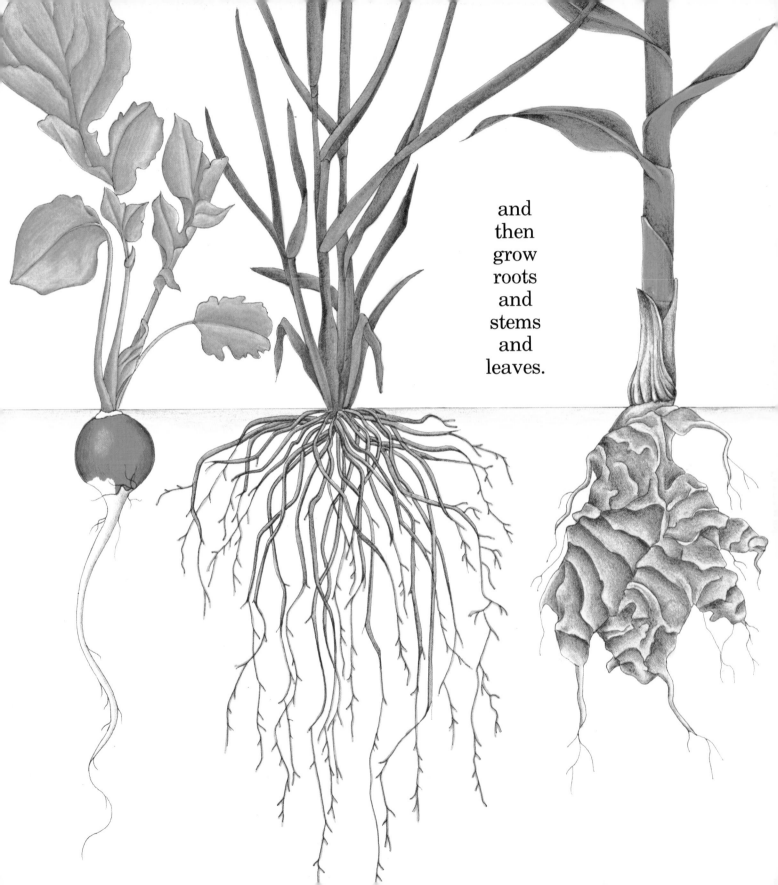

and
then
grow
roots
and
stems
and
leaves.

Some
SEEDS
grow
up

to be
TREES.

These
grow
where
it's
very
dry,

and these grow where it's wet.

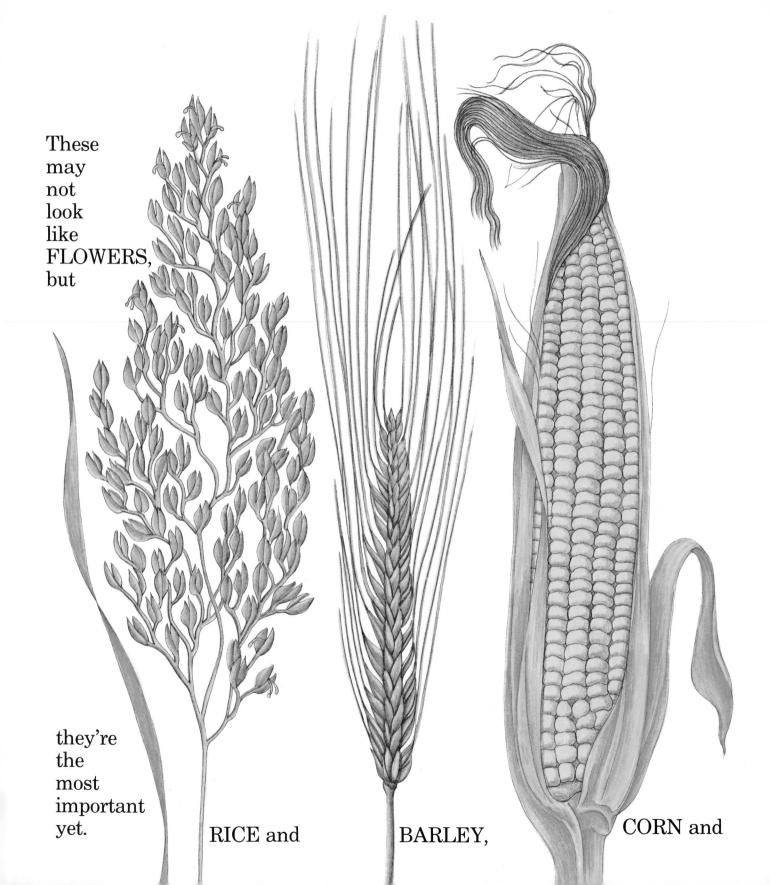

These
may
not
look
like
FLOWERS,
but

they're
the
most
important
yet.

RICE and

BARLEY,

CORN and

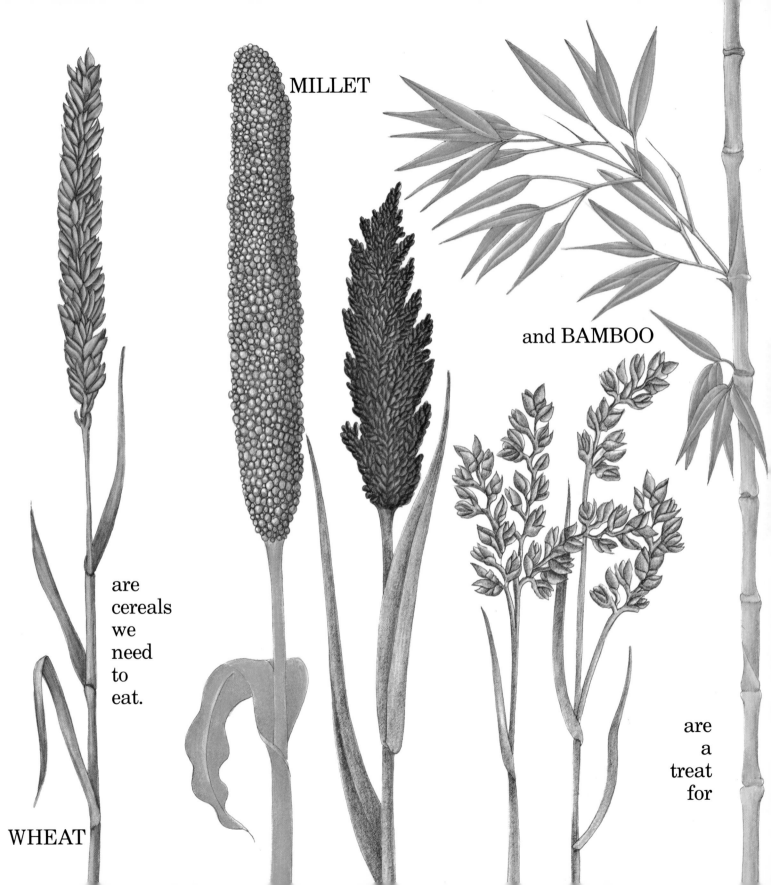

MILLET

and BAMBOO

WHEAT

are cereals we need to eat.

are a treat for

animals who don't
like meat.

They
are called
HER · BIV · O · ROUS.

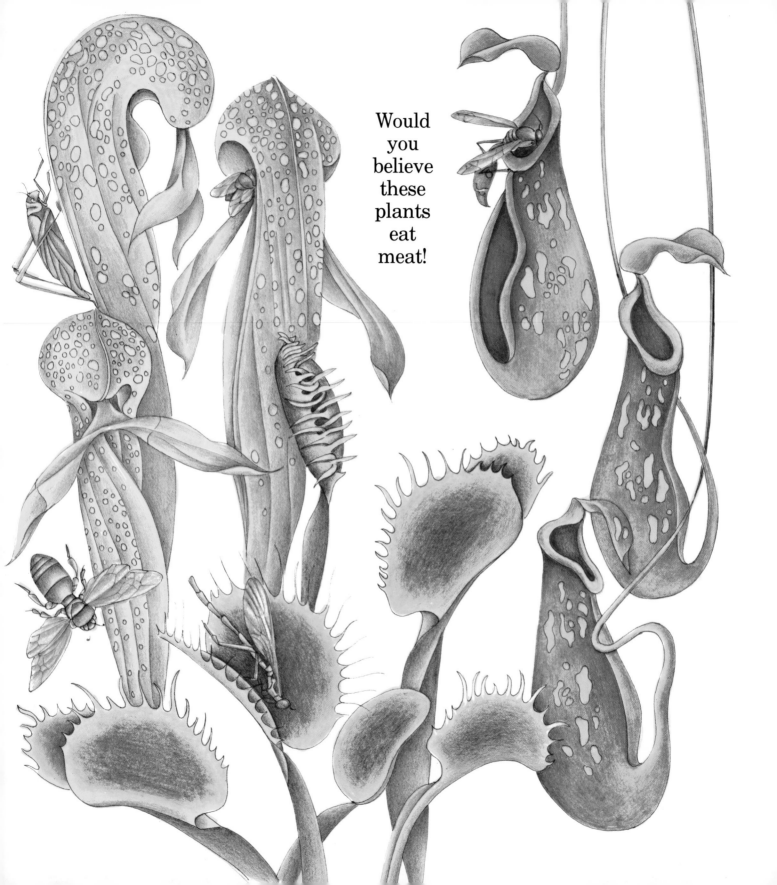

Would
you
believe
these
plants
eat
meat!

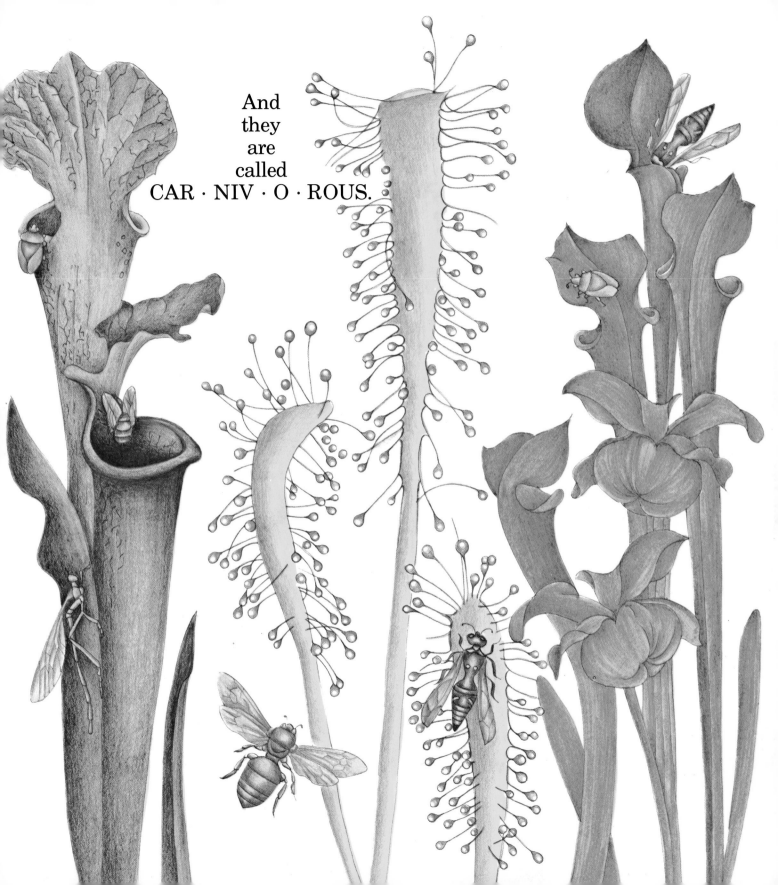

And
they
are
called
CAR · NIV · O · ROUS.

The
largest
FLOWER
ever
found
grows
in
the
jungle
near
the
ground.

A
PARASITE
clinging tight
to
roots of trees
that
feed
it,
it's three feet wide,
or
maybe four,
weighs fifteen pounds
and
sometimes more
and
has a nasty
odor.

RAFFLESIA
is its name.

But here's
a
FLOWER
that owes its fame
to
smelling very sweet,

and scientists agree
that
MAGNOLIAS
seem to be
a
prehistoric family.

Paper

Wood

Straw

Candy

Coffee

Tea

All
FLOWERS
are
AN · GIO · SPERM.

That's an ancient
Grecian
term.

Here
are
just
a very
few
products
made
from
them
for
you:

Cotton

Rope

Rubber

Perfume

Cork

Medicine

Popcorn

Pasta

Bread

Chocolate

Plants
that
have
no
flowers
are
fascinating,
too.

This one has become…

...a plum.